D1505135

Fudges, Toffees & Caramels

Fudges, Toffees & Caramels

25 foolproof recipes for the ultimate sweet treat
with 100 photographs

Claire Ptak

LORENZ BOOKS

This edition is published by
Lorenz Books, an imprint of
Anness Publishing Ltd,
Blaby Road, Wigston,
Leicestershire LE18 4SE

info@anness.com

www.lorenzbooks.com;
www.annesspublishing.com

If you like the images in this book
and would like to investigate using
them for publishing, promotions or
advertising, please visit our website
www.practicalpictures.com for
more information.

© Anness Publishing Ltd 2013

A CIP catalogue record for this book is
available from the British Library.

Publisher: Joanna Lorenz
Editor: Kate Eddison
Photographer: Nicki Dowey
Food Stylist: Claire Ptak
Food Stylist's Assistants: Kate
   McCullough and Adriana Nascimento
Prop Stylists: Wei Tang and
   Marianne de Vries
Designer: Lisa Tai
Production Controller: Ben Worley

PUBLISHER'S NOTE

Although the advice and information in this book are believed to be accurate and true
at the time of going to press, neither the authors nor the publisher can accept any legal
responsibility or liability for any errors or omissions that may have been made nor for
any inaccuracies nor for any loss, harm or injury that comes about from following
instructions or advice in this book.

NOTES

- Bracketed terms are intended for American readers.
- For all recipes, quantities are given in both metric and imperial measures and,
  where appropriate, in standard cups and spoons. Follow one set of measures,
  but not a mixture, because they are not interchangeable.
- Standard spoon and cup measures are level. 1 tsp = 5ml, 1 tbsp = 15ml,
  1 cup = 250ml/8fl oz.
- Australian standard tablespoons are 20ml. Australian readers should use 3 tsp in
  place of 1 tbsp for measuring small quantities.
- American pints are 16fl oz/2 cups. American readers should use 20fl oz/2.5 cups
  in place of 1 pint when measuring liquids.
- Electric oven temperatures in this book are for conventional ovens. When using a fan
  oven, the temperature will probably need to be reduced by about 10–20°C/20–40°F.
  Since ovens vary, you should check with your manufacturer's instruction book
  for guidance.
- The nutritional analysis given for each recipe is calculated for the total quantity.
  The analysis does not include optional ingredients, such as salt added to taste.
- Medium (US large) eggs are used unless otherwise stated.

Front cover image shows Vanilla Fudge; for recipe, see page 12.

Contents

Introduction

There are no greater confections than fudges, caramels and toffees. Whether soft and chewy or hard and suckable, their combination of sweetness and creaminess makes them utterly irresistible. Although they can be wonderful when bought from traditional stores, nothing beats the freshness of home-made varieties.

What are toffees, caramels and fudges?

Sugar, in whatever form, is the foundation of all confectionery. It can be heated with water to a range of temperatures to create different results, from hard-boiled

sweets (hard candies) to chewy taffies and soft fondants. What generally unites fudges, toffees and caramels is the addition of other ingredients, such as butter or cream.

For toffees, sugar is boiled with water to the desired colour, then butter and/or cream is added. The longer cooking time of the syrup means that toffees are characteristically harder than caramels and fudges; most toffees can be broken into pieces and sucked. The English favourite Bonfire Toffee, devoured every year on 5 November, is darkened with black treacle (molasses) to resemble the dregs of a bonfire. Other toffees, such as Honeycomb and Cinder Toffee, have

Left: Cinder Toffee is brittle with lots of air bubbles in it.

bicarbonate of soda (baking soda) added to them, which creates little air bubbles and lightens the texture.

For soft caramels, the sugar is boiled with added cream, which caramelizes at a lower temperature and is responsible for the chewy texture. Gently stirring the cooking mixture will help prevent the milk proteins from burning. Once soft caramels are poured and set, it is easy to cut them into pieces. They will keep well and are easiest to manage if they are wrapped in individual foils or squares of baking parchment. Caramel makes the perfect base for a range of flavourings, such as salt or chopped nuts, as well as coconut and fruits.

Fudge is probably the most common home-made confection. Fudge is similar to toffee and

Above: Nuts provide a lovely textural contrast to smooth, rich fudge.

caramel; it is made with precise measures of sugar, water, cream and butter. Its texture varies, and there are countless flavour combinations. During cooking, the base mixture is heated to the soft-ball stage, when vanilla, chocolate, coffee or a range of other ingredients are added. Some recipes call for beating the fudge while it is hot to give it a grainy texture. For the smoothest fudge, no stirring is required.

Essential Ingredients

There are only a few basic ingredients that you will need:

- Caster (superfine) sugar
- Full-fat (whole) milk
- Double (heavy) cream
- Unsalted butter

Extra ingredients and flavourings can include (but are not limited to):

- Granulated (white) sugar
- Demerara (raw) sugar
- Soft dark brown sugar
- Soft light brown sugar
- Bicarbonate of soda (baking soda)
- Golden (light corn) syrup
- Black treacle (molasses)
- Vanilla pods (beans)
- Vanilla extract
- Chocolate
- Nut butters
- Nuts
- Coffee
- Dried fruits
- Candied fruits
- Fruit juices
- Sea salt

Full-fat (whole) milk

Unsalted butter

Demerara (raw) sugar

Preparation tips

As with most home-made confections, toffee, caramel and fudge take time and attention, and it is vital to have ready everything you need at the start of the recipe. If you need to grease or line any tins or pans, the recipe will state this. Use either butter or

Left: Tins (pans) should be greased and lined with baking parchment.

grapeseed or groundnut (peanut) oil for greasing, as directed in the recipe. If required, you will also need to prepare an ice-water bath before starting the cooking. Having this on hand means that you can arrest the cooking as soon as the mixture reaches the desired temperature. A sugar thermometer is necessary to read temperatures, and should be placed in a jug or pitcher of warm water, ready for use.

Essential Equipment

Having the right tools will certainly make the recipes in this book easier to achieve. These are the most important things you will need:

- Copper pan
- Sugar thermometer
- Square cake tin (pan)
- Baking tray
- Wooden spoon
- Fine-meshed sieve (strainer)
- Measuring cup
- Measuring spoons
- Accurate scales

A sugar thermometer is essential.

Above: When making nut brittles, a clean rolling pin brushed with plenty of oil is a must.

Storing, wrapping or presenting your confections

If you are not eating them immediately, toffees and caramels are best wrapped individually in greaseproof or waxed paper, baking parchment, cellophane or pretty foil wrappers. You can buy sweet or candy wrappers from specialist stores or from online retailers. A sweet or candy jar with a tight-fitting lid is the best place to keep the wrapped sweets, as they will soften in the open air. Fudge does not need to be wrapped individually, but it does need to be stored in an airtight container.

Home-made confections are always popular, and they make ideal gifts at any time of year. For a nostalgic look, display them in an old-fashioned tin box, in an antique bowl or on a vintage plate. Alternatively, simply wrap them in a big square of cellophane, gathered at the top with ribbon, raffia, string or cord.

Right: There are many options when it comes to presenting your confections, whether for serving or as gifts.

Fudges and Tablets

There is an almost limitless array of recipes for fudge, but the success of them all relies on exact proportions of ingredients, cooked to the correct temperature and combined with complementary flavours. Nuts, chocolate, coffee and dried fruits are all used to create delicious fudgy morsels. A couple of lovely tablet recipes are also included here, which provide a contrast in texture. These scrummy bites make a tasty treat at any time of day and are perfect for gifts.

Vanilla Fudge

This classic recipe makes a delicious and simple fudge, which can be used as the base for a variety of different flavours. The beating of the mixture gives it its typical grainy texture. If you want the grains to be larger, stir the fudge when it is hotter.

Makes about 1kg/2¼lb

300ml/½ pint/1¼ cups
  full-fat (whole) milk
900g/2lb/4½ cups caster
  (superfine) sugar
125g/4¼oz/generous ½ cup
  unsalted butter, cut into
  1cm/½in cubes, plus extra
  for greasing
½ vanilla pod (bean)
10ml/2 tsp vanilla extract
tiny pinch of salt

Cook's Tip
Work quickly, so the fudge does not have time to seize up.

1 Grease a 20cm/8in square baking tin (pan) with butter, and line it with baking parchment. Prepare an ice-water bath.

2 Place the milk, sugar and butter in a large, heavy pan. Scrape in the vanilla seeds, then add the pod. Cook over moderate heat, stirring, until the sugar has dissolved and the butter has melted, then bring the mixture to the boil. Cover with a tight-fitting lid for 2 minutes, then remove the lid.

3 Without stirring, leave the mixture to cook at a slow rolling boil until it reaches the soft-ball stage (114°C/238°F). This will take about 10 minutes.

4 Immediately place the base of the pan in the ice-water bath for a few seconds. Discard the vanilla pod. Stir in the vanilla extract and salt.

5 Place the pan in a cool part of the kitchen until it is lukewarm or about 43°C/110°F. Do not stir. Once it reaches this temperature, beat the fudge with a wooden spoon until it is thick, smooth and creamy.

6 Pour into the prepared tin and allow to cool completely. Cut it into squares, then lift it out by the sides of the baking parchment. Serve immediately, or store in an airtight container.

Energy 4665kcal/19743kJ; Protein 15g; Carbohydrate 955g, of which sugars 955g; Fat 114g, of which saturates 75g; Cholesterol 330mg; Calcium 841mg; Fibre 0g; Sodium 1157mg

Old-fashioned Chocolate Fudge

This timeless classic is a smooth fudge that is not worked. Instead it is simply melted to the perfect temperature and poured into a tin to set. This version uses dark chocolate, which cuts through the sweetness of the sugar, but you could use milk chocolate, if you prefer.

Makes about 1.2kg/2½lb

800g/1¾lb/4 cups caster (superfine) sugar
250ml/8fl oz/1 cup full-fat (whole) milk
75g/3oz/6 tbsp unsalted butter, cut into 1cm/½in cubes, plus extra for greasing
350g/12oz dark (bittersweet) chocolate (55–60% cocoa solids), cut into small pieces
5ml/1 tsp vanilla extract

1 Grease a 20 x 30cm/8 x 12in rectangular baking tin (pan) with butter, and line it with baking parchment. Prepare an ice-water bath.

2 Put the sugar, milk and butter in a large, heavy pan and cook over a medium heat, stirring constantly, until the sugar has dissolved.

3 When the sugar has dissolved and the butter has melted, stop stirring. Bring the mixture to the boil.

4 Without stirring, let the mixture cook at a slow rolling boil until it reaches the soft-ball stage (114°C/238°F). This will take about 10 minutes. Stir in the chocolate.

5 Immediately place the base of the pan in the ice-water bath for a few seconds. Stir in the vanilla extract.

6 Pour the mixture into the prepared baking tin. Leave to cool completely.

7 Lift the fudge out of the tin by the sides of the baking parchment, and place it on a cutting surface. Cut it into squares. Serve immediately, or store in an airtight container.

Cook's Tip
If you want the fudge to have a grainier texture, you can stir it with a spoon while it cools down. (*See* the recipe for Vanilla Fudge, page 12.)

Energy 5707kcal/24098kJ; Protein 29g; Carbohydrate 1075g, of which sugars 1056g; Fat 173g, of which saturates 105g; Cholesterol 239mg; Calcium 856mg; Fibre 0g; Sodium 787mg

Almond Milk Fudge

This fudge is inspired by the Indian sweets that are popular in restaurants all over the world. Clarified butter adds a nutty flavour, and ground almonds give the fudge a grainy texture. The edible silver leaf is an optional finishing touch that makes it look really special.

Makes about 800g/1¾lb

115g/4oz/½ cup unsalted butter, plus extra for greasing
500ml/17fl oz/generous 2 cups double (heavy) cream
175g/6oz/scant 1 cup caster (superfine) sugar
500g/1¼lb/5 cups ground almonds
edible silver leaf (optional)

Variation
You could add a little orange blossom water or rose water to the mixture as well, to make these more flavourful, but the simplicity of almonds, cream, sugar and butter is lovely.

1 Begin by clarifying the butter. Place the butter in a small pan on the lowest heat. Leave it to melt without disturbing it, then skim any white foam off the top. Pour the yellow, 'clarified' liquid into a jar, leaving any white milk solids behind. Do not worry about leaving a tiny amount of the fat in the pan if it means keeping the clarified butter completely free from the milk solids. You may not need all of the clarified butter, but whatever you do not use can be kept in an airtight container in the refrigerator for 2 weeks.

2 Grease a 20cm/8in square baking tin (pan) with butter, and line it with baking parchment.

3 Place the cream in a heavy pan over medium heat, bring to the boil and boil for 10 minutes.

4 Add the sugar and stir until dissolved. Add the ground almonds and 50g/2oz of the clarified butter. Stir constantly for 5 minutes.

5 Pour the mixture into the prepared tin and press down with a palette knife or offset metal spatula. Cover with a sheet of baking parchment and weight it down with a block of wood (such as a chopping board) and some weights. Leave to cool for 10 minutes.

6 Remove the board and the top layer of baking parchment. Lift the fudge from the tin using the edges of the baking parchment. Decorate the surface with edible silver leaf, if you like, using a clean paint brush or pastry brush to transfer the leaf from the paper to the fudge.

7 While the fudge is still slightly warm, cut it into diamond shapes. Leave to cool completely, then remove from the tin. Serve immediately or store in an airtight container.

Energy 6842kcal/28342kJ; Protein 116g; Carbohydrate 231g, of which sugars 217g; Fat 642g, of which saturates 236g; Cholesterol 915mg; Calcium 1560mg; Fibre 37g; Sodium 1128mg

Peanut Butter Fudge

This fudge has a fabulous texture. The combination of smooth, creamy peanut butter and melted milk chocolate result in a silkiness that cannot be attained any other way. Use a high-quality natural peanut butter with no added sugars or fats.

Makes about 1.3kg/3lb

750g/1lb 11oz/3¾ cups caster (superfine) sugar
250ml/8fl oz/generous 1 cup golden (light corn) syrup
300ml/½ pint/1¼ cups double (heavy) cream
75g/3oz/6 tbsp unsalted butter, cut into 1cm/½in cubes, plus extra for greasing
200g/7oz/scant 1 cup smooth peanut butter
150g/5oz/scant 1 cup roasted and salted peanuts, chopped
100g/3¾oz milk chocolate, chopped

1 Grease a 20cm/8in square baking tin (pan) with butter, and line it with baking parchment.

2 Put the sugar, golden syrup, cream and butter in a large, heavy pan, and cook over medium heat, stirring constantly, until the sugar dissolves.

3 When the sugar has dissolved and the butter has melted, bring the mixture to the boil.

4 Without stirring, let the mixture cook at a slow rolling boil until it reaches the soft-ball stage (114°C/238°F). This will take about 10 minutes.

5 Remove the pan from the heat and stir in the peanut butter. Fold in the nuts and chocolate.

6 Pour the mixture into the prepared tin, and allow it to cool completely. This can take up to 8 hours.

7 Lift the fudge out of the tin by the sides of the baking parchment, and place it on a cutting surface. Cut the fudge into squares. Serve immediately or store in an airtight container.

Variation
For a different consistency, use crunchy peanut butter instead of smooth.

Energy 8274kcal/34696kJ; Protein 97g; Carbohydrate 1091g, of which sugars 1068g; Fat 435g, of which saturates 185g; Cholesterol 572mg; Calcium 791mg; Fibre 19.8g; Sodium 2705mg

Espresso and Macadamia Fudge

Macadamia nuts make the perfect partner for fudge, as their oily yet slightly crunchy texture complements the creaminess of the fudge. The addition of coffee extract is merely to give it a little lift. Use the freshest nuts possible, as macadamia nuts have a short shelf life.

Makes about 1.3kg/3lb

750g/1lb 11oz/3¾ cups caster (superfine) sugar
250ml/8fl oz/generous 1 cup golden (light corn) syrup
300ml/½ pint/1¼ cups double (heavy) cream
375g/13oz milk chocolate, chopped
250g/9oz macadamia nuts, chopped
75g/3oz/6 tbsp unsalted butter, cut into 1cm/½in cubes, plus extra for greasing
5ml/1 tsp coffee extract or instant espresso powder, dissolved in 10ml/2 tsp boiling water

1 Grease a 20 x 30cm/8 x 12in rectangular baking tin (pan) with butter, and line it with baking parchment, making sure the paper comes right up the sides of the tin.
2 Place the sugar, golden syrup and cream in a large, heavy pan, and cook over moderate heat, stirring constantly, until the sugar has dissolved.
3 When the sugar has dissolved, bring the mixture to the boil.
4 Without stirring, let the mixture cook at a slow rolling boil until it reaches the soft-ball stage (114°C/238°F). This will take about 10 minutes.
5 Remove from the heat and quickly stir in the chocolate, nuts, butter, and coffee extract or espresso. Keep stirring until the chocolate and butter have completely melted and are thoroughly combined.
6 Pour the fudge mixture into the prepared baking tin, and leave it to cool completely. This can take up to 8 hours.
7 Lift the fudge out of the tin by the sides of the baking parchment, and place it on a cutting surface. Cut the fudge into squares. Serve immediately or store in an airtight container.

Energy 9614kcal/40330kJ; Protein 134g; Carbohydrate 1257g, of which sugars 1224g; Fat 502g, of which saturates 227g; Cholesterol 675mg; Calcium 1665mg; Fibre 22g; Sodium 1851mg

Candied Clementine Fudge

Divine nuggets of beautiful candied clementine peel make this fudge truly special. You will need to go to a speciality delicatessen or a department store with a food hall to obtain candied clementine peel. Alternatively, you can use candied orange or lemon peel instead.

Makes about 1.3kg/3lb

750g/1lb 11oz/3¾ cups caster (superfine) sugar
50ml/2fl oz/¼ cup golden (light corn) syrup
300ml/½ pint/1¼ cups double (heavy) cream
100g/3¾oz/scant ½ cup unsalted butter, cut into 1cm/½in cubes, plus extra for greasing
15ml/1 tbsp grated clementine rind
350g/12oz white chocolate, chopped
150g/5oz/¾ cup candied clementine peel, chopped
30ml/2 tbsp clementine juice
30ml/2 tbsp lemon juice

1 Grease a 20 x 30cm/8 x 12in baking tin (pan) with butter, and line it with baking parchment.
2 Put the sugar, golden syrup, cream, butter and clementine rind in a large, heavy pan, and cook over moderate heat, stirring to dissolve the sugar.
3 When the sugar has dissolved and the butter has melted, bring the mixture to the boil and, without stirring, let the mixture cook at a slow rolling boil until it reaches the soft-ball stage (114°C/238°F). This will take about 10 minutes.
4 Remove the pan from the heat and stir in the white chocolate, two-thirds of the candied clementine peel, the clementine juice and the lemon juice. Pour the fudge mixture into the prepared baking tin.
5 Sprinkle over the remaining peel and allow to cool completely. This can take up to 8 hours.
6 Lift the fudge out of the tin by the sides of the paper and cut it into squares. Serve immediately, or store in an airtight container.

Energy 7450kcal/31305kJ; Protein 38.9g; Carbohydrate 1132.5g, of which sugars 1132.5g; Fat 355.4g, of which saturates 209.5g; Cholesterol 620mg; Calcium 1746mg; Fibre 7.2g; Sodium 1860mg

Penuche Fudge

This is an old-fashioned fudge in which the key ingredient is brown or raw sugar (in Spanish, 'panocha' means raw sugar). You can experiment with different raw and brown sugars until you find the taste you like best. The sugar is what gives the fudge its signature caramel taste.

Makes about 675g/1½lb

400g/14oz/1¾ cups soft dark brown sugar
100ml/3½fl oz/scant ½ cup golden (light corn) syrup
225ml/7½fl oz/scant 1 cup double (heavy) cream
50g/2oz/4 tbsp unsalted butter, cut into 1cm/½in cubes, plus extra for greasing
200g/7oz/1¼ cups walnuts, chopped
7.5ml/1½ tsp vanilla extract

Variation

Walnuts are used here, but pecans are equally delicious and make the fudge reminiscent of pecan praline.

1 Grease a 20cm/8in square baking tin (pan) with butter, and line it with baking parchment, making sure the paper comes right up the sides of the tin. Prepare an ice-water bath.

2 Put the sugar, golden syrup, cream and butter in a large, heavy pan, and cook over a medium heat, stirring constantly, until the sugar has dissolved.

3 When the sugar has dissolved and the butter has melted, bring the mixture to the boil.

4 Without stirring, let the mixture cook at a slow rolling boil until it reaches the soft-ball stage (114°C/238°F). This will take about 10 minutes.

5 Remove from the heat and dip the base of the pan into the ice-water bath. Set aside to cool until it is lukewarm (about 50°C/122°F).

6 Stir in the nuts and vanilla extract, and beat until creamy. Pour into the prepared tin, smooth the surface and leave to cool completely.

7 Lift the fudge out of the tin with the sides of the paper, and place on a cutting surface. Cut it into squares. Serve immediately, or store in an airtight container.

Energy 4611kcal/19281kJ; Protein 34g; Carbohydrate 495g, of which sugars 493g; Fat 299g, of which saturates 113g; Cholesterol 423mg; Calcium 546mg; Fibre 12g; Sodium 1463mg

Yogurt Pecan Fudge

This delectable treat is similar to penuche fudge, in which brown sugar is the main flavouring. In this modern twist, yogurt is used in place of double (heavy) cream for a lighter, tangier flavour. Do not use Greek (US strained plain) yogurt in this recipe.

Makes about 550g/1lb 4oz

225ml/7½fl oz/scant 1 cup natural (plain) yogurt
5ml/1 tsp bicarbonate of soda (baking soda)
400g/14oz/1¾ cups soft light brown sugar
30ml/2 tbsp golden (light corn) syrup
60g/2½oz/5 tbsp unsalted butter, plus extra for greasing
150g/5oz/1 cup chopped, toasted pecans

1 Combine the yogurt and bicarbonate of soda in a large, heavy pan, and set aside for 20 minutes.

2 Meanwhile, grease a 20cm/8in square baking tin (pan) with butter, and line it with baking parchment. Prepare an ice-water bath.

3 Add the soft light brown sugar and golden syrup to the yogurt mixture, then cook over medium heat, stirring, until the sugar has dissolved.

4 Bring the mixture to the boil and then add the butter. Boil until the syrup reaches the soft-ball stage (114°C/238°F).

5 Remove from the heat, and dip the base of the pan into the ice-water bath for a few seconds. Set aside and leave to cool until the mixture is lukewarm (about 50°C/122°F).

6 Beat the fudge until creamy, then stir in the chopped, toasted pecans. Pour the mixture into the prepared tin, and leave to cool completely.

7 Lift the fudge out of the tin by the sides of the baking parchment, and cut into thin wedges. Serve immediately, or store in an airtight container.

Energy 3267kcal/13719kJ; Protein 27.7g; Carbohydrate 467.3g, of which sugars 465g; Fat 156.4g, of which saturates 42.1g; Cholesterol 141mg; Calcium 748mg; Fibre 7g; Sodium 743mg

Rocky Road Fudge

Most often associated with ice cream, rocky road is a classic American treat. An impressive way to present this fudge is to put it into a loaf tin and then slice it like a terrine when it is set. The fudge can be cut into smaller pieces, if you prefer.

Makes about 3kg/6¾ lb

75g/3oz/½ cup walnuts, roughly chopped

1.4kg/3lb 2oz/7 cups caster (superfine) sugar

500ml/17fl oz/generous 2 cups full-fat (whole) milk

150g/5oz/10 tbsp unsalted butter, cut into 1cm/½in cubes

700g/1lb 11oz dark (bittersweet) chocolate (55–60% cocoa solids), cut into small pieces

10ml/2 tsp vanilla extract

1.5ml/¼ tsp salt

130g/4½oz mini marshmallows (or large marshmallows, cut into pieces)

90g/3½oz amarena cherries or sour cherries in syrup, sliced in half

1 Line a 10 x 23cm/4 x 9in loaf tin (pan) with clear film (plastic wrap) so that it comes out of the tin and over the sides.

2 Place the sugar, milk and butter in a medium, heavy pan. Cook over moderate heat, stirring constantly, until the sugar has dissolved and the butter has melted, then bring the mixture to the boil. Without stirring, allow it to cook at a slow rolling boil until it reaches the soft-ball stage (114°C/238°F). This will take about 10 minutes. Stir in the chocolate, vanilla extract and salt.

3 Pour one-third of the mixture into the prepared baking tin. Sprinkle with one-third of the marshmallows and half of the cherries and walnuts. Cover with half of the remaining fudge. Sprinkle with the rest of the cherries and walnuts, and half of the remaining marshmallows. Cover with the rest of the fudge mixture and sprinkle over the remaining marshmallows.

4 Place a piece of baking parchment over the top and press it down firmly with your hands. Set aside to cool completely.

5 Remove the fudge from the tin by holding the sides of the clear film, and cut it into 1cm/½in slices. Serve immediately, or store in an airtight container.

Energy 11632kcal/49052kJ; Protein 73.2g; Carbohydrate 2067.8g, of which sugars 2006g; Fat 397.8g, of which saturates 215.5g; Cholesterol 478mg; Calcium 1695mg; Fibre 3.2g; Sodium 1611mg

Vanilla Tablet

Tablet is a hybrid of fudge and toffee that dates back to 18th-century Scotland. It has a grainy texture, similar to fudge, but is harder. Traditionally it was made using just sugar and cream, but since this has a tendency to burn, this recipe includes sweetened condensed milk.

Makes about 1kg/2¼lb

900g/2lb/4½ cups caster (superfine) sugar
125g/4¼oz/generous ½ cup unsalted butter, plus extra for greasing
150ml/¼ pint/⅔ cup water
150ml/¼ pint/⅔ cup full-fat (whole) milk
1 vanilla pod (bean)
200ml/7fl oz/scant 1 cup sweetened condensed milk

Cook's Tip
Versions of tablet are made all over the world. In Quebec it is called *sucre à la crème* and is made with maple syrup; in South America it is called *tableta de leche*; and it is known as *borstplaat* in the Netherlands.

1 Grease a 20cm/8in square baking tin (pan) or 23cm/9in square baking dish with butter, and line it with baking parchment.
2 Combine the sugar, butter, water and milk in a heavy pan over low heat.
3 Split the vanilla pod down the centre, and scrape the seeds from inside using a small knife. Add the seeds and the pod to the pan. Stir gently until the sugar has dissolved and the butter has melted, then turn the heat up to medium and bring to the boil. Do not stir at this point.
4 Boil the mixture until it reaches the soft-ball stage (114°C/238°F), then stir in the condensed milk. Bring the mixture back up to 114°C/238°F, then remove the pan from the heat. Leave the tablet mixture to cool for 5 minutes, then remove the vanilla pod with a fork, and discard.
5 Using a wooden spoon, stir the mixture vigorously for a few minutes until creamy and lighter in colour. Pour the mixture into the tin through a sieve (strainer). Leave to cool completely, then turn it out on to a board, and cut it into squares. Serve immediately, or store in an airtight container.

Energy 5232kcal/22142kJ; Protein 26.9g; Carbohydrate 1058.7g, of which sugars 1058.7g; Fat 128.2g, of which saturates 83.7g; Cholesterol 381mg; Calcium 1248mg; Fibre 0g; Sodium 1354mg

Fig Tablet

This recipe has a wonderful texture: fudgy tablet bursting with chopped fig and vanilla seeds. Tablet works well with any dried fruit – try dried apricots or prunes, if you like. Do not use fresh figs, as they hold too much juice and the tablet will not set properly.

Makes about 1.3kg/3lb

100g/3¾oz/⅔ cups dried
  figs, chopped
150ml/¼ pint/⅔ cup full-fat
  (whole) milk
50g/2oz/¼ cup unsalted butter,
  plus extra for greasing
2.5ml/½ tsp salt
900g/2lb/4½ cups caster
  (superfine) or granulated
  (white) sugar
1 vanilla pod (bean)

Variations
• Use desiccated (dry unsweetened shredded) coconut instead of figs, and add 15ml/1 tbsp Bacardi rum or Malibu.
• Use 10ml/2 tsp vanilla extract in place of the seeds of the vanilla pod, for a more economical recipe.

1 Grease a 20cm/8in square baking tin (pan) or 23cm/9in square baking dish with butter, and line it with baking parchment. Place the figs in a bowl, and cover with 50ml/2fl oz/¼ cup boiling water. Leave to soak for 30 minutes.
2 Put 150ml/¼ pint/⅔ cup water in a large, heavy pan with the milk, butter, salt and sugar, and place over low heat. Stir to combine. Split the vanilla pod down the centre. Scrape the seeds into the pan, and add the pod.
3 Stir gently until the sugar has dissolved and the butter has melted, then turn the heat up to medium and bring the mixture to the boil. Boil the mixture until it reaches the soft-ball stage (114°C/238°F).
4 Meanwhile, strain the figs and pat them dry using kitchen paper. As soon as the syrup has reached the soft-ball stage, stir in the figs. Remove from the heat and leave to cool for 5 minutes. Remove the vanilla pod, and discard.
5 Using a wooden spoon, stir the syrup vigorously for a few minutes until creamy and lighter in colour. Pour the tablet mixture into the prepared tin, and leave to cool completely. Turn the tablet out on to a board, and cut it into squares. Serve immediately, or store in an airtight container.

Energy 4223kcal/17946kJ; Protein 12.9g; Carbohydrate 996.3g, of which sugars 996.3g; Fat 48.2g, of which saturates 30.6g; Cholesterol 136mg; Calcium 887mg; Fibre 6.9g; Sodium 569mg

Caramels, Toffees and Nut Brittles

An amazing range of textures can be achieved when sugar is combined with other ingredients, such as butter, cream and golden syrup, and heated to a specific temperature. From chewy toffees to firmer butterscotch and light-as-air honeycomb, there is sure to be something for everyone in this chapter. Delicious on their own, these treats can be further enhanced by the addition of chocolate, nuts or seeds, or embellished with gold leaf for an extra-special touch.

Pecan Toffees

This rich, deep and dark toffee recipe comes originally from New Orleans. Its French-Creole name is La Colle, which means 'glue'; when made correctly, it should have a luxuriously thick and very smooth texture, interspersed with crunchy pecans.

Makes about 550g/1lb 5oz

125g/4¼oz/¾ cup pecans
50ml/2fl oz/¼ cup water
425g/15oz/scant 2 cups soft
dark brown sugar

Variation
Substitute the soft dark brown sugar with black treacle (molasses), but use only 225g/8oz/²⁄₃ cup.

1 Preheat the oven to 160°C/325°F/Gas 3. Spread the pecans out on a baking sheet and place in the oven. Set the timer for 7 minutes.

2 After 7 minutes, check the nuts, giving them a toss. They will probably need another few minutes. Test whether they are done by breaking one in half. It should be slightly golden but not brown and have a toasted aroma.

3 Remove the pecans from the oven. Allow them to cool for a few minutes, then transfer them to a chopping board. Chop the pecans roughly, then sift them to separate the fine powder from the nut pieces. Set them both aside.

4 Place the water into a heavy pan, add the soft dark brown sugar and heat over low heat until the sugar has dissolved completely.

5 Once the sugar has dissolved, turn the heat up to medium-high and bring the mixture to the boil. Boil until it reaches the soft-crack stage (143°C/290°F).

6 Stir in the toasted, chopped pecans. Spoon the mixture into mini cake or petit-four cases, then sprinkle with the fine nut powder. Leave to cool completely. Serve immediately or store them in an airtight container.

Energy 2536kcal/10698kJ; Protein 13.6g; Carbohydrate 451.4g, of which sugars 449.5g; Fat 87.6g, of which saturates 7.1g; Cholesterol 0mg; Calcium 302mg; Fibre 5.9g; Sodium 27mg

Salted Caramels

These extra-dark caramels have the wonderful crunch of sea salt. Although it may be a surprising addition to the confection, salted caramels are becoming increasingly popular. The salt cuts the sweetness of the caramel and creates a lovely balance.

Makes about 1kg/2¼lb

450ml/¾ pint/scant 2 cups double (heavy) cream
1 vanilla pod (bean), split down the side
225g/8oz/⅔ cup golden (light corn) syrup
400g/14oz/2 cups caster (superfine) or granulated (white) sugar
65g/2½oz/⅓ cup unsalted butter
7.5ml/1½ tsp fleur de sel or other fine sea salt

Variation
Play around with the types of salt you use. Fleur de sel is suggested in the recipe, but Maldon sea salt is also an interesting choice.

1   Line a 23cm/9in square cake tin (pan) with baking parchment, so that the paper comes up the sides of the tin on all sides.

2   Gently heat the cream in a heavy pan. Scrape the seeds from the vanilla pod and add them, along with the pod, to the cream.

3   Bring the cream and vanilla to just under the boil, being careful not to scorch it. When it is ready, it will start to exude wisps of steam and have a thin layer of frothy foam beginning to form at the edges of the pan.

4   In another heavy pan, heat the golden syrup and sugar gently until the sugar dissolves, then bring to the boil. Boil until it reaches the hard-crack stage (154°C/310°F).

5   Once the cream has heated to the required stage, strain it through a sieve (strainer), discarding the vanilla pod.

6   Add the butter, 5ml/1 tsp salt and the strained cream to the sugar mixture. Stir just enough to combine the ingredients, then bring the whole mixture back up to the firm-ball stage (120°C/248°F).

7   Pour the caramel mixture into the prepared tin, and tamp it down on the work surface to release any air bubbles. Sprinkle the remaining salt over the surface.

8   Leave the caramel to cool completely for a few hours, then take hold of the sides of the paper and lift the caramel block out of the tin. Cut it into bitesize rectangles using a sharp knife.

9   Wrap the caramels individually in foil squares. Serve immediately, or store in an airtight container at room temperature. They will keep for about 10 days.

Energy 4746kcal/19870kJ; Protein 11g; Carbohydrate 608g, of which sugars 608g; Fat 295g, of which saturates 170g; Cholesterol 735mg; Calcium 505mg; Fibre 0g; Sodium 1286mg

Caramel and Pecan Chews

These extra-dark caramels are silky and chewy, with the added crunch of toasted pecans. They are almost like a bitesize pecan pie without the pastry. Pecans are native to the southern United States and they make a natural pairing with caramelized sugar.

Makes 48

450ml/¾ pint/scant 2 cups double (heavy) cream
1 vanilla pod (bean), split down the side
225g/8oz/⅔ cup golden (light corn) syrup
400g/14oz/2 cups granulated (white) sugar
65g/2½oz/⅓ cup unsalted butter
5ml/1 tsp fleur de sel or other fine sea salt
100g/3¾oz/scant 1 cup toasted, chopped pecans
edible gold leaf (optional)

Cook's Tip
Use unlined foil cases, if possible, to prevent the caramels from sticking.

1 Arrange 48 mini foil sweet cases on two baking sheets. Set aside.
2 Gently heat the cream in a heavy pan. Scrape the seeds from the vanilla pod and add to the cream, along with the pod.
3 Bring the cream to just under the boil, being careful not to scorch it. When it is ready, it will exude wisps of steam and have a thin layer of frothy foam forming at the edges of the pan.
4 In another heavy pan, heat the golden syrup and sugar gently until the sugar dissolves, then boil until it reaches the hard-crack stage (154°C/310°F).
5 When the cream has reached the required temperature, strain it through a sieve (strainer), discarding the vanilla pod.
6 Add the butter, salt and the strained cream to the sugar mixture. Stir to combine only, then bring it back up to the firm-ball stage (120°C/248°F).
7 Stir in the toasted, chopped pecans. Spoon the caramel into the foil cases, then gently tap the baking sheet on the work surface to release any air bubbles. Leave to cool completely. Serve immediately or store in an airtight container for about 10 days.

Energy 113kcal/473kJ; Protein 0.4g; Carbohydrate 12.8g, of which sugars 12.8g; Fat 7.6g, of which saturates 3.7g; Cholesterol 15mg; Calcium 12mg; Fibre 0.1g; Sodium 27mg

Fresh Coconut and Cardamom Caramels

This might seem like an unusual flavour combination, but it works very well. The texture of fresh coconut suspended in chewy caramel is a lovely surprise, while the distinctive flavour of the cardamom cuts through the sweetness. The rum adds the finishing touch!

Makes about 1kg/2¼lb

freshly grated flesh of 1 coconut
500g/1¼lb/2½ cups caster
  (superfine) sugar
200ml/7fl oz/scant 1 cup golden
  (light corn) syrup
225ml/7½fl oz/scant 1 cup
  double (heavy) cream
50g/2oz/¼ cup unsalted butter,
  cut into small cubes,
  plus extra for greasing
1.5ml/¼ tsp ground cardamom
10ml/2 tsp white rum

1 Grease a 20 x 30cm/8 x 12in baking tin (pan) with butter, and line it with baking parchment.

2 Heat a large, heavy pan and drop the grated coconut into it, in batches, stirring until it is dry and flaky. Transfer the coconut to a bowl, and set aside.

3 Place the sugar, golden syrup and cream in a heavy pan set over medium heat, and stir to dissolve the sugar. Add the butter, cardamom and coconut, and stir to melt the butter.

4 When the butter has melted, bring the pan to the boil and, without stirring, let the mixture cook at a slow rolling boil for about 10 minutes, or until it reaches the soft-ball stage (114°C/238°F).

5 Remove the pan from the heat and stir in the rum. Pour the mixture into the prepared tin, and leave to cool completely. This can take up to 8 hours.

6 Turn the caramel out on to a board, and cut it into squares. Wrap them individually in waxed paper or foil candy wrappers. Serve immediately, or store in an airtight container at room temperature for up to 10 days.

Energy 4419kcal/18575kJ; Protein 12g; Carbohydrate 692g, of which sugars 692g; Fat 208g, of which saturates 135g; Cholesterol 408mg; Calcium 454mg; Fibre 10g; Sodium 1049mg

Nutty Chocolate Toffee

This toffee is crunchy and buttery, and could be made with any one of your favourite nuts.
The combination of dark chocolate and macadamia works wonderfully, making this treat rich
and luxurious. Different nuts, such as pecans or hazelnuts, would be equally delicious.

Makes about 850g/1lb 12oz

200g/7oz/generous 1 cup
  macadamia nut halves
60ml/4 tbsp water
350g/12oz/1¾ cups caster
  (superfine) sugar
125g/4¼oz/8½ tbsp
  unsalted butter
15ml/1 tbsp black treacle
  (molasses)
1.5ml/¼ tsp sea salt
5ml/1 tsp vanilla extract
1.5ml/¼ tsp bicarbonate of
  soda (baking soda)
150g/5oz dark (bittersweet)
  chocolate (60–70% cocoa
  solids), finely chopped

1 Preheat the oven to 160°C/325°F/Gas 3. Spread the macadamias out on
a baking sheet and place in the oven. Set a timer for 5 minutes, then check
the nuts, giving them a toss. They will probably need a few minutes more.
They should be golden but not brown. Remove from the oven. Set aside.

2 Line a shallow baking tray with baking parchment. Spread three-quarters
of the macadamias out on the tray, tightly packed so they cover the bottom.

3 Combine the water, sugar, butter, black treacle and salt in a heavy pan.
Place over low heat, and heat until the sugar has dissolved.

4 Bring to the boil. Boil, without stirring, until the syrup reaches the hard-
crack stage (154°C/310°F). Immediately remove from the heat, and stir in
the vanilla and bicarbonate of soda, until thoroughly incorporated.

5 Pour the mixture over the nuts. Shake the tray and tap it on the counter,
then sprinkle the chocolate on top (the chocolate will melt into the toffee).

6 Roughly chop the reserved nuts, and sprinkle them on the chocolate.
Leave to cool completely, then break into pieces. Serve immediately or store
in an airtight container.

Energy 4254kcal/17814kJ; Protein 61g; Carbohydrate 498g, of which sugars 478g; Fat 238g, of which saturates 109g; Cholesterol 301mg;
Calcium 456mg; Fibre 12g; Sodium 993mg

Bonfire Toffee

Dark, intensely flavoured and satisfyingly brittle to crunch on, this traditional British toffee is the perfect accompaniment to fireworks and fun on Bonfire Night. It tastes strongly of black treacle, but the flavour is rounded by the demerara sugar and the richness of the butter.

Makes about 600g/1lb 6oz

125g/4¼oz/8½ tbsp unsalted butter, plus extra for greasing
225ml/7½fl oz/scant 1 cup black treacle (molasses)
200g/7oz/scant 1 cup demerara (raw) sugar
tiny pinch of salt

1 Grease a shallow baking tray with butter.
2 Place the butter in a large, heavy pan, and set it over low heat until it has melted.
3 Add the black treacle and demerara sugar and, still over low heat, let them gently dissolve into the butter.
4 Once the sugar has dissolved, turn the heat up to medium, and bring the mixture to the boil. Boil until the mixture is just below the hard-crack stage (140°C/280°F).
5 Immediately pour the syrup into the prepared baking tray. Leave it to cool and harden for about 10 minutes.
6 When the toffee is completely cold, break it into bitesize shards using a palette knife (metal spatula).
7 Serve the bonfire toffee immediately, or wrap each shard individually in squares of greaseproof or waxed paper, and store them in an airtight container.

Energy 2386kcal/10037kJ; Protein 4.5g; Carbohydrate 386g, of which sugars 386g; Fat 102g, of which saturates 68g; Cholesterol 288mg; Calcium 1263mg; Fibre 0g; Sodium 1167mg

Cinder Toffee

Like golden cinders from the fire, this toffee is an old favourite in many parts of the world. It is known by many names, including yellow man, puff candy, hokey pokey, sponge candy, sea foam and angel food candy.

Makes about 300g/11oz

butter, for greasing
60ml/4 tbsp water
225g/8oz/generous 1 cup
  caster (superfine) sugar
15ml/1 tbsp golden
  (light corn) syrup
1.5ml/¼ tsp bicarbonate of
  soda (baking soda), sifted
5ml/1 tsp warm water

Cook's Tip
To make this into an extra-special treat, dip the toffee pieces into melted chocolate and allow them to set.

1   Prepare an ice-water bath and a jug (pitcher) of warm water large enough to hold your sugar thermometer. Grease a shallow baking tray with butter, and set it aside.

2   Place the water in a heavy pan, and add the sugar and golden syrup. Heat gently until the sugar has dissolved.

3   Increase the heat, and bring to the boil, then boil, without stirring, until it is just above the hard-crack stage (154°C/310°F) and takes on a little colour.

4   Remove the thermometer, and place it in the jug of warm water. Remove the syrup from the heat and place it over the ice-water bath to arrest the cooking.

5   Dissolve the bicarbonate of soda in the warm water, then pour it into the sugar syrup. At this point, it will bubble and froth up, so take great care.

6   Quickly stir the mixture to disperse the bubbles, then pour the mixture into the prepared baking tray, and leave to cool and harden.

7   When cooled, break into pieces. Serve immediately, or wrap the shards in cellophane, or greaseproof or waxed paper, and store in an airtight container.

Energy 931kcal/3973kJ; Protein 1.2g; Carbohydrate 247g, of which sugars 247g; Fat 0g, of which saturates 0g; Cholesterol 0mg; Calcium 123mg; Fibre 0g; Sodium 54mg

Honeycomb Toffee

Equally traditional, this is a richer version of honeycomb than Cinder Toffee. To make it lighter in colour and taste, you can replace the black treacle with honey. The bicarbonate of soda gives this its light, airy texture. Be sure to sift it before adding it in to avoid lumps.

Makes about 750g/1lb 13oz

125g/4¼oz/generous ½ cup unsalted butter, plus extra for greasing
30ml/2 tbsp cider vinegar or white wine vinegar
100ml/3½fl oz/scant ½ cup black treacle (molasses)
200ml/7fl oz/scant 1 cup golden (light corn) syrup
400g/14oz/1¾ cups demerara (raw) sugar
2.5ml/½ tsp bicarbonate of soda (baking soda), sifted

1 Grease a 20cm/8in square cake tin (pan) with butter. Line it with baking parchment so that the paper comes up the sides of the tin.
2 Melt the butter gently in a large, heavy pan over a low heat. Add the vinegar, black treacle, golden syrup and demerara sugar. Stir gently until the sugar has dissolved into the butter.
3 Turn the heat up to medium then, without stirring, heat the syrup until it reaches the hard-crack stage (154°C/310°F).
4 Remove the pan from the heat and immediately stir in the sifted bicarbonate of soda. As the mixture begins to froth, stir it once again. Take great care as the hot syrup bubbles up.
5 Pour the mixture into the prepared tin, and leave it to cool. When it begins to set (after 30 minutes), score the toffee with a knife into bitesize squares.
6 Leave it to cool completely for a few hours before taking hold of the sides of the paper and lifting the block out of the tin. Break into squares along the scored lines. Store in an airtight container.

Energy 3350kcal/14147kJ; Protein 4.4g; Carbohydrate 643g, of which sugars 643g; Fat 102g, of which saturates 68g; Cholesterol 288mg; Calcium 783mg; Fibre 0g; Sodium 1598mg

Burnt Caramel Shards

A very different method for making toffee, this recipe does not require a sugar thermometer. Gold leaf is expensive, but it makes the caramel shards look beautiful. You could crush the caramel to make a crunchy ice cream topping, in which case, do not bother with the gold leaf.

Makes about 400g/14oz

100g/3¾oz/scant ½ cup unsalted butter, plus extra for greasing
300g/11oz/1½ cups caster (superfine) sugar
2 sheets of edible loose gold leaf (optional)

Cook's Tip
Edible gold leaf can come in two different forms: loose leaf or pressed to paper. Loose gold leaf, used here, should be applied with a clean, dry paint or pastry brush. Gently lift pieces from between the sheets of paper and lower it on to the surface you want to cover with the gold. Pressed gold leaf should be rubbed on to the caramel by inverting the paper on to it and rubbing it with your finger.

1 Grease a baking tray with butter, and set it aside.

2 Place the butter in a heavy pan, and melt it gently over low heat. Add the sugar.

3 Increase the heat to medium, and stir the butter and sugar mixture constantly using a wooden spoon until it has become a dark caramel colour; this will take about 10 minutes. The sugar and butter may separate during the cooking process, but they should come back together again in an emulsified mass by the time the caramel mixture is the right colour.

4 Carefully pour the caramel mixture on to the prepared baking tray, and leave to cool.

5 Apply the gold leaf (if using) to the surface of the caramel using a clean, dry paint or pastry brush. (*See* Cook's Tip.)

6 Once the toffee is completely cool and hard, break it into shards. Serve immediately, or wrap the pieces individually in cellophane, or greaseproof or waxed paper, and store in an airtight container.

Energy 1919kcal/8074kJ; Protein 2g; Carbohydrate 314g, of which sugars 314g; Fat 82g, of which saturates 54g; Cholesterol 230mg;; Calcium 174mg; Fibre 0g; Sodium 768mg

Butterscotch

Depending on who you talk to you will get a very different answer for the question of which is the most traditional of all sweets, but butterscotch will certainly be a popular choice. This recipe is similar to a caramel, but the syrup is cooked a little longer to get a more brittle result.

Makes about 800g/1¾lb

400g/14oz/2 cups caster (superfine) or granulated (white) sugar
150ml/1¼ pint/⅔ cup double (heavy) cream
150ml/¼ pint/⅔ cup water
1 vanilla pod (bean), split down the side
1.5ml/¼ tsp cream of tartar
100g/3¾oz/scant ½ cup unsalted butter, cut into small cubes, plus extra for greasing

1   Grease a 20cm/8in square cake tin (pan) with butter, and line it with baking parchment so that the paper comes all the way up the sides.
2   Place the sugar, cream and water in a heavy pan over low heat, and stir gently until the sugar has dissolved.
3   Scrape the vanilla seeds from the pod into the pan, then add the pod as well. Add the cream of tartar. Increase the heat to medium, and boil until it reaches the soft-ball stage (114°C/238°F).
4   Add the butter. Boil until it reaches the soft-crack stage (143°C/290°F).
5   Pour the mixture into the prepared tin, retrieving and discarding the vanilla pod.
6   Let it cool slightly, then score the top to make it easy to break into squares when it has cooled.
7   When it is completely cold, break it into squares and wrap them in greaseproof or waxed paper, cellophane or foils. Serve immediately, or store in an airtight container at room temperature for up to 10 days.

Variation

For chocolate butterscotch, add 15ml/1 tbsp cocoa powder to the pan with the sugar, cream and water.

Energy 2987kcal/12529kJ; Protein 5g; Carbohydrate 422g, of which sugars 422g; Fat 162g, of which saturates 99g; Cholesterol 425mg; Calcium 302mg; Fibre 0g; Sodium 830mg

Peanut Brittle

It is the addition of bicarbonate of soda that gives brittle its unique texture. It introduces thousands of tiny air bubbles into the sugar syrup, making it crunchy and airy. The stretching process also adds air and gives the brittle an almost opalescent quality.

Makes 600g/1lb 6oz

grapeseed or groundnut (peanut)
  oil, for greasing
175g/6oz/scant 1 cup caster
  (superfine) sugar
115g/4oz/⅓ cup golden
  (light corn) syrup
5ml/1 tsp salt
250g/9oz/1½ cups raw peanuts
25g/1oz/2 tbsp unsalted
  butter, cubed
2.5ml/½ tsp vanilla extract
2.5ml/½ tsp bicarbonate of soda
  (baking soda)

1 Line a baking sheet with parchment, and grease it lightly with oil.

2 Combine the sugar, golden syrup and salt with 60ml/4 tbsp water in a large, heavy pan. Heat the mixture gently over low heat until the sugar has dissolved.

3 Turn the heat up to medium, and boil until the syrup reaches the hard-ball stage (130°C/266°F).

4 Add the peanuts and stir until the syrup reaches the hard-crack stage (154°C/310°F). Transfer the mixture to a heatproof bowl, and stir in the butter and vanilla.

5 Dissolve the bicarbonate of soda in 5ml/1 tsp warm water, and fold into the peanut mixture. Pour the mixture out on to the prepared baking sheet.

6 Leave the mixture until it is cool enough to touch, then, with oiled hands, pull the brittle from the sides to stretch it and make holes.

7 Leave the brittle to cool completely, before breaking it up with the back of a spoon. Serve immediately, or store in an airtight container for a few days at room temperature.

Energy 2626kcal/11011kJ; Protein 65g; Carbohydrate 305g, of which sugars 289g; Fat 135g, of which saturates 34g; Cholesterol 58mg; Calcium 276mg; Fibre 16g; Sodium 514mg

Pistachio Cracknel

Honey makes an excellent partner for pistachios. Native to the Middle East, pistachios have been a food source for thousands of years. This cracknel is wonderful sprinkled over ice cream in the summer, or folded into whipped cream for a rich accompaniment to a winter pudding.

Makes about 350g/12oz

grapeseed or groundnut (peanut) oil, for greasing
175g/6oz/scant 1 cup caster (superfine) sugar
75g/3oz/⅓ cup clear honey
100g/3¾oz/⅓ cup pistachios, shelled

1 Grease a marble slab or baking sheet and a rolling pin with oil. Set them aside.

2 Dissolve the sugar and honey in a heavy pan over medium heat, stirring constantly.

3   Add the pistachios, increase the heat to bring the mixture to the boil, then boil until the mixture reaches the hard-crack stage (154°C/310°F), stirring occasionally.

4 Pour the cracknel mixture out on to the oiled marble slab or baking sheet, and roll it flat using the oiled rolling pin.

5 Leave the cracknel to cool until it is cool enough to touch, then, with oiled hands, pull the cracknel from the sides to stretch it and make holes.

6 Leave it to cool completely, then break the cracknel into pieces using the back of a spoon. Serve immediately, or store in an airtight container for a few days at room temperature.

Energy 1507kcal/6347kJ; Protein 18g; Carbohydrate 249g, of which sugars 247g; Fat 55g, of which saturates 7g; Cholesterol 7mg; Calcium 131mg; Fibre 0g; Sodium 547mg

Hazelnut Praline

The key to this delectable recipe is toasting the hazelnuts to perfection. Make sure you set the oven timer, then keep checking them regularly, if they are not done. This recipe makes a classic praline that can be processed to a powder and sprinkled over ice cream.

Makes 600g/1lb 6oz

200g/7oz/1¼ cups whole
  hazelnuts, with skins
butter, for greasing
60ml/4 tbsp water
400g/14oz/2 cups caster
  (superfine) sugar
1.5ml/¼ tsp cream of tartar

Cook's Tip
Always buy the freshest hazelnuts you can and use them quickly. It is best to buy them with the skins on as they have better flavour.

1 Preheat the oven to 180°C/350°F/Gas 4. Spread the hazelnuts out on a baking sheet so that they are all in one layer. Place them in the oven, and set a timer for 7 minutes, then check them. They should have a golden colour and firm texture. Cook them for a little longer, if necessary.

2 Empty the nuts into a clean dish towel and, while still warm, rub the nuts with the towel until the skins have all come off.

3 Grease a sheet of baking parchment with butter, and use it to line the bottom of a baking tray. Transfer the skinned nuts on to it in a single layer.

4 Combine the water, sugar and cream of tartar in a heavy pan. Place over medium heat and bring to the boil, stirring to dissolve the sugar.

5 Once the sugar has dissolved, stop stirring and bring to the boil. Boil the syrup until it reaches the hard-crack stage (154°C/310°F), then continue cooking for 1 minute more. Immediately pour the syrup over the nuts.

6 Allow the caramel to cool completely, before breaking it into bitesize pieces using your hands. Serve immediately, or store in an airtight container. It can also be processed to a fine powder and sprinkled over ice cream.

Energy 2876kcal/12094kJ; Protein 30.2g; Carbohydrate 430g, of which sugars 426g; Fat 127g, of which saturates 9.4g; Cholesterol 0mg; Calcium 492mg; Fibre 13g; Sodium 36mg

Salty Cashew Croccante

This crunchy croccante could be made with any of your favourite nuts, but the classic salty-sweet combination of cashew nuts and toffee works especially well in this recipe. Ensure you use fresh, raw, unsalted cashews rather than salted ones, or the croccante will be too salty.

Makes about 425g/15oz

grapeseed or groundnut (peanut)
  oil, for greasing
200g/7oz/1¼ cups raw unsalted
  cashew nuts
60ml/4 tbsp water
200g/7oz/1 cup caster
  (superfine) sugar
25g/1oz/2 tbsp butter, cubed
2.5ml/½ tsp sea salt

1   Preheat the oven to 180°C/350°F/Gas 4. Grease a marble slab and a rolling pin with oil.

2   Spread the cashew nuts out on a baking sheet and cook them in the preheated oven for about 7 minutes, or until the cashews are very lightly toasted. Watch them closely so that they do not burn.

3   Meanwhile, combine the water and sugar in a heavy pan. Place over low heat until the sugar dissolves and the syrup starts to colour. Stir in the hot cashews. Continue to cook, stirring constantly, until the syrup reaches the hottest soft-crack stage (143°C/290°F).

4   Remove the pan from the heat, and stir in the butter. Pour the mixture out on to the oiled marble. Roll the oiled rolling pin over it to flatten it out.

5   Sprinkle the surface lightly with the sea salt and then allow the croccante to cool until it is cool enough to touch.

6   Stretch it out with oiled hands. Leave to cool completely, then break it into pieces. Serve immediately or store in an airtight container.

Energy 2121kcal/889kJ; Protein 36g; Carbohydrate 246g, of which sugars 219g; Fat 117g, of which saturates 33g; Cholesterol 58mg; Calcium 94mg; Fibre 0g; Sodium 1010mg

Index